THE WHISTLEBLOWER FILE

COMPLETE TEXT OF:

1. The Whistleblower complaint as submitted to the United States Congress

2. The Inspector General's letter to the Acting Director of Intelligence regarding the complaint

3. The text of the phone conversation between President Trump and President Zelensky of Ukraine

4. All tweets by President Trump from September 21, 2019 (7:31 am) to September 26 (11:48 pm)

These are documents as they were released by various US agencies to the public after being declassified.

President Trump's tweets were taken from public records and are presented as they were tweeted without any selection process being applied.

This reproduction is published by
Arc Manor, LLC

978-1-61242-474-3

CONTENTS

1. The Whistleblower complaint as submitted to the United States Congress

August 12, 2019

The Honorable Richard Burr
Chairman
Select Committee on Intelligence
United States Senate

The Honorable Adam Schiff
Chairman
Permanent Select Committee on Intelligence
United States House of Representatives

Dear Chairman Burr and Chairman Schiff:

I am reporting an "urgent concern" in accordance with the procedures outlined in 50 U.S.C. §3033(k)(5)(A). This letter is UNCLASSIFIED when separated from the attachment.

In the course of my official duties, I have received information from multiple U.S. Government officials that the President of the United States is using the power of his office to solicit interference from a foreign country in the 2020 U.S. election. This interference includes, among other things, pressuring a foreign country to investigate one of the President's main domestic political rivals. The President's personal lawyer, Mr. Rudolph Giuliani, is a central figure in this effort. Attorney General Barr appears to be involved as well.

- Over the past four months, more than half a dozen U.S. officials have informed me of various facts related to this effort. The information provided herein was relayed to me in the course of official interagency business. It is routine for U.S. officials with responsibility for a particular regional or functional portfolio to share such information with one another in order to inform policymaking and analysis.
- I was not a direct witness to most of the events described. However, I found my colleagues' accounts of these events to be credible because, in almost all cases, multiple officials recounted fact patterns that were consistent with one another. In addition, a variety of information consistent with these private accounts has been reported publicly.

I am deeply concerned that the actions described below constitute "a serious or flagrant problem, abuse, or violation of law or Executive Order" that "does not include differences of opinions concerning public policy matters," consistent with the definition of an "urgent concern" in 50 U.S.C. §3033(k)(5)(G). I am therefore fulfilling my duty to report this information, through proper legal channels, to the relevant authorities.

- I am also concerned that these actions pose risks to U.S. national security and undermine the U.S. Government's efforts to deter and counter foreign interference in U.S. elections.

UNCLASSIFIED

To the best of my knowledge, the entirety of this statement is unclassified when separated from the classified enclosure. I have endeavored to apply the classification standards outlined in Executive Order (EO) 13526 and to separate out information that I know or have reason to believe is classified for national security purposes.[1]

- If a classification marking is applied retroactively, I believe it is incumbent upon the classifying authority to explain why such a marking was applied, and to which specific information it pertains.

I.   The 25 July Presidential phone call

Early in the morning of 25 July, the President spoke by telephone with Ukrainian President Volodymyr Zelenskyy. I do not know which side initiated the call. This was the first publicly acknowledged call between the two leaders since a brief congratulatory call after Mr. Zelenskyy won the presidency on 21 April.

Multiple White House officials with direct knowledge of the call informed me that, after an initial exchange of pleasantries, the President used the remainder of the call to advance his personal interests. Namely, he sought to pressure the Ukrainian leader to take actions to help the President's 2020 reelection bid. According to the White House officials who had direct knowledge of the call, the President pressured Mr. Zelenskyy to, inter alia:

- initiate or continue an investigation[2] into the activities of former Vice President Joseph Biden and his son, Hunter Biden;
- assist in purportedly uncovering that allegations of Russian interference in the 2016 U.S. presidential election originated in Ukraine, with a specific request that the Ukrainian leader locate and turn over servers used by the Democratic National Committee (DNC) and examined by the U.S. cyber security firm Crowdstrike,[3] which initially reported that Russian hackers had penetrated the DNC's networks in 2016; and
- meet or speak with two people the President named explicitly as his personal envoys on these matters, Mr. Giuliani and Attorney General Barr, to whom the President referred multiple times in tandem.

---

[1] Apart from the information in the Enclosure, it is my belief that none of the information contained herein meets the definition of "classified information" outlined in EO 13526, Part 1, Section 1.1. There is ample open-source information about the efforts I describe below, including statements by the President and Mr. Giuliani. In addition, based on my personal observations, there is discretion with respect to the classification of private comments by or instructions from the President, including his communications with foreign leaders; information that is not related to U.S. foreign policy or national security—such as the information contained in this document, when separated from the Enclosure—is generally treated as unclassified. I also believe that applying a classification marking to this information would violate EO 13526, Part 1, Section 1.7, which states: "In no case shall information be classified, continue to be maintained as classified, or fail to be declassified in order to: (1) conceal violations of law, inefficiency, or administrative error; [or] (2) prevent embarrassment to a person, organization, or agency."

[2] It is unclear whether such a Ukrainian investigation exists. See Footnote #7 for additional information.

[3] I do not know why the President associates these servers with Ukraine. (See, for example, his comments to *Fox News* on 20 July: "And Ukraine. Take a look at Ukraine. How come the FBI didn't take this server? Podesta told them to get out. He said, get out. So, how come the FBI didn't take the server from the DNC?")

2
UNCLASSIFIED

The President also praised Ukraine's Prosecutor General, Mr. Yuriy Lutsenko, and suggested that Mr. Zelenskyy might want to keep him in his position. (Note: Starting in March 2019, Mr. Lutsenko made a series of public allegations—many of which he later walked back—about the Biden family's activities in Ukraine, Ukrainian officials' purported involvement in the 2016 U.S. election, and the activities of the U.S. Embassy in Kyiv. See Part IV for additional context.)

The White House officials who told me this information were deeply disturbed by what had transpired in the phone call. They told me that there was already a "discussion ongoing" with White House lawyers about how to treat the call because of the likelihood, in the officials' retelling, that they had witnessed the President abuse his office for personal gain.

The Ukrainian side was the first to publicly acknowledge the phone call. On the evening of 25 July, a readout was posted on the website of the Ukrainian President that contained the following line (translation from original Russian-language readout):

- "Donald Trump expressed his conviction that the new Ukrainian government will be able to quickly improve Ukraine's image and complete the investigation of corruption cases that have held back cooperation between Ukraine and the United States."

Aside from the above-mentioned "cases" purportedly dealing with the Biden family and the 2016 U.S. election, I was told by White House officials that no other "cases" were discussed.

Based on my understanding, there were approximately a dozen White House officials who listened to the call—a mixture of policy officials and duty officers in the White House Situation Room, as is customary. The officials I spoke with told me that participation in the call had not been restricted in advance because everyone expected it would be a "routine" call with a foreign leader. I do not know whether anyone was physically present with the President during the call.

- In addition to White House personnel, I was told that a State Department official, Mr. T. Ulrich Brechbuhl, also listened in on the call.
- I was not the only non-White House official to receive a readout of the call. Based on my understanding, multiple State Department and Intelligence Community officials were also briefed on the contents of the call as outlined above.

II.   Efforts to restrict access to records related to the call

In the days following the phone call, I learned from multiple U.S. officials that senior White House officials had intervened to "lock down" all records of the phone call, especially the official word-for-word transcript of the call that was produced—as is customary—by the White House Situation Room. This set of actions underscored to me that White House officials understood the gravity of what had transpired in the call.

- White House officials told me that they were "directed" by White House lawyers to remove the electronic transcript from the computer system in which such transcripts are typically stored for coordination, finalization, and distribution to Cabinet-level officials.

- Instead, the transcript was loaded into a separate electronic system that is otherwise used to store and handle classified information of an especially sensitive nature. One White House official described this act as an abuse of this electronic system because the call did not contain anything remotely sensitive from a national security perspective.

I do not know whether similar measures were taken to restrict access to other records of the call, such as contemporaneous handwritten notes taken by those who listened in.

III.   Ongoing concerns

On 26 July, a day after the call, U.S. Special Representative for Ukraine Negotiations Kurt Volker visited Kyiv and met with President Zelenskyy and a variety of Ukrainian political figures. Ambassador Volker was accompanied in his meetings by U.S. Ambassador to the European Union Gordon Sondland. Based on multiple readouts of these meetings recounted to me by various U.S. officials, Ambassadors Volker and Sondland reportedly provided advice to the Ukrainian leadership about how to "navigate" the demands that the President had made of Mr. Zelenskyy.

I also learned from multiple U.S. officials that, on or about 2 August, Mr. Giuliani reportedly traveled to Madrid to meet with one of President Zelenskyy's advisers, Andriy Yermak. The U.S. officials characterized this meeting, which was not reported publicly at the time, as a "direct follow-up" to the President's call with Mr. Zelenskyy about the "cases" they had discussed.

- Separately, multiple U.S. officials told me that Mr. Giuliani had reportedly privately reached out to a variety of other Zelenskyy advisers, including Chief of Staff Andriy Bohdan and Acting Chairman of the Security Service of Ukraine Ivan Bakanov.[4]
- I do not know whether those officials met or spoke with Mr. Giuliani, but I was told separately by multiple U.S. officials that Mr. Yermak and Mr. Bakanov intended to travel to Washington in mid-August.

On 9 August, the President told reporters: "I think [President Zelenskyy] is going to make a deal with President Putin, and he will be invited to the White House. And we look forward to seeing him. He's already been invited to the White House, and he wants to come. And I think he will. He's a very reasonable guy. He wants to see peace in Ukraine, and I think he will be coming very soon, actually."

IV.   Circumstances leading up to the 25 July Presidential phone call

Beginning in late March 2019, a series of articles appeared in an online publication called *The Hill*. In these articles, several Ukrainian officials—most notably, Prosecutor General Yuriy Lutsenko—made a series of allegations against other Ukrainian officials and current and former U.S. officials. Mr. Lutsenko and his colleagues alleged, inter alia:

---

[4] In a report published by the Organized Crime and Corruption Reporting Project (OCCRP) on 22 July, two associates of Mr. Giuliani reportedly traveled to Kyiv in May 2019 and met with Mr. Bakanov and another close Zelenskyy adviser, Mr. Serhiy Shefir.

- that they possessed evidence that Ukrainian officials—namely, Head of the National Anticorruption Bureau of Ukraine Artem Sytnyk and Member of Parliament Serhiy Leshchenko—had "interfered" in the 2016 U.S. presidential election, allegedly in collaboration with the DNC and the U.S. Embassy in Kyiv;[5]
- that the U.S. Embassy in Kyiv—specifically, U.S. Ambassador Marie Yovanovitch, who had criticized Mr. Lutsenko's organization for its poor record on fighting corruption—had allegedly obstructed Ukrainian law enforcement agencies' pursuit of corruption cases, including by providing a "do not prosecute" list, and had blocked Ukrainian prosecutors from traveling to the United States expressly to prevent them from delivering their "evidence" about the 2016 U.S. election;[6] and
- that former Vice President Biden had pressured former Ukrainian President Petro Poroshenko in 2016 to fire then Ukrainian Prosecutor General Viktor Shokin in order to quash a purported criminal probe into Burisma Holdings, a Ukrainian energy company on whose board the former Vice President's son, Hunter, sat.[7]

In several public comments,[8] Mr. Lutsenko also stated that he wished to communicate directly with Attorney General Barr on these matters.[9]

The allegations by Mr. Lutsenko came on the eve of the first round of Ukraine's presidential election on 31 March. By that time, Mr. Lutsenko's political patron, President Poroshenko, was trailing Mr. Zelenskyy in the polls and appeared likely to be defeated. Mr. Zelenskyy had made known his desire to replace Mr. Lutsenko as Prosecutor General. On 21 April, Mr. Poroshenko lost the runoff to Mr. Zelenskyy by a landslide. See Enclosure for additional information.

---

[5] Mr. Sytnyk and Mr. Leshchenko are two of Mr. Lutsenko's main domestic rivals. Mr. Lutsenko has no legal training and has been widely criticized in Ukraine for politicizing criminal probes and using his tenure as Prosecutor General to protect corrupt Ukrainian officials. He has publicly feuded with Mr. Sytnyk, who heads Ukraine's only competent anticorruption body, and with Mr. Leshchenko, a former investigative journalist who has repeatedly criticized Mr. Lutsenko's record. In December 2018, a Ukrainian court upheld a complaint by a Member of Parliament, Mr. Boryslav Rozenblat, who alleged that Mr. Sytnyk and Mr. Leshchenko had "interfered" in the 2016 U.S. election by publicizing a document detailing corrupt payments made by former Ukrainian President Viktor Yanukovych before his ouster in 2014. Mr. Rozenblat had originally filed the motion in late 2017 after attempting to flee Ukraine amid an investigation into his taking of a large bribe. On 16 July 2019, Mr. Leshchenko publicly stated that a Ukrainian court had overturned the lower court's decision.
[6] Mr. Lutsenko later told Ukrainian news outlet *The Babel* on 17 April that Ambassador Yovanovitch had never provided such a list, and that he was, in fact, the one who requested such a list.
[7] Mr. Lutsenko later told *Bloomberg* on 16 May that former Vice President Biden and his son were not subject to any current Ukrainian investigations, and that he had no evidence against them. Other senior Ukrainian officials also contested his original allegations; one former senior Ukrainian prosecutor told *Bloomberg* on 7 May that Mr. Shokin in fact was not investigating Burisma at the time of his removal in 2016.
[8] See, for example, Mr. Lutsenko's comments to *The Hill* on 1 and 7 April and his interview with *The Babel* on 17 April, in which he stated that he had spoken with Mr. Giuliani about arranging contact with Attorney General Barr.
[9] In May, Attorney General Barr announced that he was initiating a probe into the "origins" of the Russia investigation. According to the above-referenced OCCRP report (22 July), two associates of Mr. Giuliani claimed to be working with Ukrainian officials to uncover information that would become part of this inquiry. In an interview with *Fox News* on 8 August, Mr. Giuliani claimed that Mr. John Durham, whom Attorney General Barr designated to lead this probe, was "spending a lot of time in Europe" because he was "investigating Ukraine." I do not know the extent to which, if at all, Mr. Giuliani is directly coordinating his efforts on Ukraine with Attorney General Barr or Mr. Durham.

- It was also publicly reported that Mr. Giuliani had met on at least two occasions with Mr. Lutsenko: once in New York in late January and again in Warsaw in mid-February. In addition, it was publicly reported that Mr. Giuliani had spoken in late 2018 to former Prosecutor General Shokin, in a Skype call arranged by two associates of Mr. Giuliani.[10]
- On 25 April in an interview with *Fox News*, the President called Mr. Lutsenko's claims "big" and "incredible" and stated that the Attorney General "would want to see this."

On or about 29 April, I learned from U.S. officials with direct knowledge of the situation that Ambassador Yovanovitch had been suddenly recalled to Washington by senior State Department officials for "consultations" and would most likely be removed from her position.

- Around the same time, I also learned from a U.S. official that "associates" of Mr. Giuliani were trying to make contact with the incoming Zelenskyy team.[11]
- On 6 May, the State Department announced that Ambassador Yovanovitch would be ending her assignment in Kyiv "as planned."
- However, several U.S. officials told me that, in fact, her tour was curtailed because of pressure stemming from Mr. Lutsenko's allegations. Mr. Giuliani subsequently stated in an interview with a Ukrainian journalist published on 14 May that Ambassador Yovanovitch was "removed...because she was part of the efforts against the President."

On 9 May, *The New York Times* reported that Mr. Giuliani planned to travel to Ukraine to press the Ukrainian government to pursue investigations that would help the President in his 2020 reelection bid.

- In his multitude of public statements leading up to and in the wake of the publication of this article, Mr. Giuliani confirmed that he was focused on encouraging Ukrainian authorities to pursue investigations into alleged Ukrainian interference in the 2016 U.S. election and alleged wrongdoing by the Biden family.[12]
- On the afternoon of 10 May, the President stated in an interview with *Politico* that he planned to speak with Mr. Giuliani about the trip.
- A few hours later, Mr. Giuliani publicly canceled his trip, claiming that Mr. Zelenskyy was "surrounded by enemies of the [U.S.] President...and of the United States."

On 11 May, Mr. Lutsenko met for two hours with President-elect Zelenskyy, according to a public account given several days later by Mr. Lutsenko. Mr. Lutsenko publicly stated that he had told Mr. Zelenskyy that he wished to remain as Prosecutor General.

---

[10] See, for example, the above-referenced articles in *Bloomberg* (16 May) and OCCRP (22 July).

[11] I do not know whether these associates of Mr. Giuliani were the same individuals named in the 22 July report by OCCRP, referenced above.

[12] See, for example, Mr. Giuliani's appearance on *Fox News* on 6 April and his tweets on 23 April and 10 May. In his interview with *The New York Times*, Mr. Giuliani stated that the President "basically knows what I'm doing, sure, as his lawyer." Mr. Giuliani also stated: "We're not meddling in an election, we're meddling in an investigation, which we have a right to do... There's nothing illegal about it... Somebody could say it's improper. And this isn't foreign policy – I'm asking them to do an investigation that they're doing already and that other people are telling them to stop. And I'm going to give them reasons why they shouldn't stop it because that information will be very, very helpful to my client, and may turn out to be helpful to my government."

Starting in mid-May, I heard from multiple U.S. officials that they were deeply concerned by what they viewed as Mr. Giuliani's circumvention of national security decisionmaking processes to engage with Ukrainian officials and relay messages back and forth between Kyiv and the President. These officials also told me:

- that State Department officials, including Ambassadors Volker and Sondland, had spoken with Mr. Giuliani in an attempt to "contain the damage" to U.S. national security; and
- that Ambassadors Volker and Sondland during this time period met with members of the new Ukrainian administration and, in addition to discussing policy matters, sought to help Ukrainian leaders understand and respond to the differing messages they were receiving from official U.S. channels on the one hand, and from Mr. Giuliani on the other.

During this same timeframe, multiple U.S. officials told me that the Ukrainian leadership was led to believe that a meeting or phone call between the President and President Zelenskyy would depend on whether Zelenskyy showed willingness to "play ball" on the issues that had been publicly aired by Mr. Lutsenko and Mr. Giuliani. (Note: This was the general understanding of the state of affairs as conveyed to me by U.S. officials from late May into early July. I do not know who delivered this message to the Ukrainian leadership, or when.) See Enclosure for additional information.

Shortly after President Zelenskyy's inauguration, it was publicly reported that Mr. Giuliani met with two other Ukrainian officials: Ukraine's Special Anticorruption Prosecutor, Mr. Nazar Kholodnytskyy, and a former Ukrainian diplomat named Andriy Telizhenko. Both Mr. Kholodnytskyy and Mr. Telizhenko are allies of Mr. Lutsenko and made similar allegations in the above-mentioned series of articles in *The Hill*.

On 13 June, the President told *ABC*'s George Stephanopoulos that he would accept damaging information on his political rivals from a foreign government.

On 21 June, Mr. Giuliani tweeted: "New Pres of Ukraine still silent on investigation of Ukrainian interference in 2016 and alleged Biden bribery of Poroshenko. Time for leadership and investigate both if you want to purge how Ukraine was abused by Hillary and Clinton people."

In mid-July, I learned of a sudden change of policy with respect to U.S. assistance for Ukraine. See Enclosure for additional information.

ENCLOSURE: Classified appendix

August 12, 2019

(U) CLASSIFIED APPENDIX

(U) Supplementary classified information is provided as follows:

(U) Additional information related to Section II

(TS/██████) According to multiple White House officials I spoke with, the transcript of the President's call with President Zelenskyy was placed into a computer system managed directly by the National Security Council (NSC) Directorate for Intelligence Programs. This is a standalone computer system reserved for codeword-level intelligence information, such as covert action. According to information I received from White House officials, some officials voiced concerns internally that this would be an abuse of the system and was not consistent with the responsibilities of the Directorate for Intelligence Programs. According to White House officials I spoke with, this was "not the first time" under this Administration that a Presidential transcript was placed into this codeword-level system solely for the purpose of protecting politically sensitive—rather than national security sensitive—information.

(U) Additional information related to Section IV

Information Relating To Classified Intelligence Community Reporting & Analysis

██

(S/██) I would like to expand upon two issues mentioned in Section IV that might have a connection with the overall effort to pressure the Ukrainian leadership. As I do not know definitively whether the below-mentioned decisions are connected to the broader efforts I describe, I have chosen to include them in the classified annex. If they indeed represent genuine policy deliberations and decisions formulated to advance U.S. foreign policy and national security, one might be able to make a reasonable case that the facts are classified.

- (S/██) I learned from U.S. officials that, on or around 14 May, the President instructed Vice President Pence to cancel his planned travel to Ukraine to attend President

Information Relating to Classified Intelligence Community Reporting & Analysis

██

Zelenskyy's inauguration on 20 May; Secretary of Energy Rick Perry led the delegation instead. According to these officials, it was also "made clear" to them that the President did not want to meet with Mr. Zelenskyy until he saw how Zelenskyy "chose to act" in office. I do not know how this guidance was communicated, or by whom. I also do not know whether this action was connected with the broader understanding, described in the unclassified letter, that a meeting or phone call between the President and President Zelenskyy would depend on whether Zelenskyy showed willingness to "play ball" on the issues that had been publicly aired by Mr. Lutsenko and Mr. Giuliani.

- (S/██) On 18 July, an Office of Management and Budget (OMB) official informed Departments and Agencies that the President "earlier that month" had issued instructions to suspend all U.S. security assistance to Ukraine. Neither OMB nor the NSC staff knew why this instruction had been issued. During interagency meetings on 23 July and 26 July, OMB officials again stated explicitly that the instruction to suspend this assistance had come directly from the President, but they still were unaware of a policy rationale. As of early August, I heard from U.S. officials that some Ukrainian officials were aware that U.S. aid might be in jeopardy, but I do not know how or when they learned of it.

2. The Inspector General's letter to the Acting Director of Intelligence regarding the complaint

OFFICE OF THE INSPECTOR GENERAL OF THE INTELLIGENCE COMMUNITY
WASHINGTON, D.C. 20511

This Letter is ~~TOP SECRET~~/████████████ **when detached from the Enclosures**

August 26, 2019

VIA HAND DELIVERY

The Honorable Joseph Maguire
Director of National Intelligence (Acting)
Office of the Director of National Intelligence
Washington, D.C. 20511

Dear Acting Director Maguire:

(U) On Monday, August 12, 2019, the Office of the Inspector General of the Intelligence Community (ICIG) received information from an individual (hereinafter, the "Complainant") concerning an alleged "urgent concern," pursuant to 50 U.S.C. § 3033(k)(5)(A). The law requires that, "[n]ot later than the end of the 14-calendar-day period beginning on the date of receipt from an employee of a complaint or information under subparagraph A, the Inspector General shall determine whether the complaint or information appears credible."[1] For the reasons discussed below, among others, I have determined that the Complainant has reported an "urgent concern" that "appears credible."

(U) As you know, the ICIG is authorized to, among other things, "receive and investigate . . . complaints or information from any person concerning the existence of an activity within the authorities and responsibilities of the Director of National Intelligence constituting a violation of laws, rules, or regulations, or mismanagement, gross waste of funds, abuse of authority, or a substantial and specific danger to the public health and safety."[2] In connection with that authority, "[a]n employee of an element of the intelligence community, an employee assigned or detailed to an element of the intelligence community, or an employee of a contractor to the intelligence community who intends to report to Congress a complaint or information with respect to an urgent concern may report such complaint or information" to the ICIG.[3]

Classified By: ███████████
Derived From:
Declassify On:

---

[1] (U) *Id.* at § 3033(k)(5)(B).

[2] (U) *Id.* at § 3033(g)(3).

[3] (U) *Id.* at § 3033(k)(5)(A).

(U) The term "urgent concern" is defined, in relevant part, as:

> (U) A serious or flagrant problem, abuse, violation of law or Executive order, or deficiency relating to the funding, administration, or operation of an intelligence activity within the responsibility and authority of the Director of National Intelligence involving classified information, but does not include differences of opinions concerning public policy matters.[4]

(U//FOUO) The Complainant's identity is known to me. As allowed by law, however, the Complainant has requested that the ICIG not disclose the Complainant's identity at this time.[5] For your information, the Complainant has retained an attorney, identified the attorney to the ICIG, and requested that the attorney be the Complainant's point of contact in subsequent communications with the congressional intelligence committees on this matter.

(U//FOUO) As part of the Complainant's report to the ICIG of information with respect to the urgent concern, the Complainant included a letter addressed to The Honorable Richard Burr, Chairman, U.S. Senate Select Committee on Intelligence, and The Honorable Adam Schiff, Chairman, U.S. House of Representatives Permanent Select Committee on Intelligence (hereinafter, the "Complainant's Letter"). The Complainant's Letter referenced a separate, Classified Appendix containing information pertaining to the urgent concern (hereinafter, the "Classified Appendix"), which the Complainant also provided to the ICIG and which the Complainant intends to provide to Chairmen Burr and Schiff. The ICIG attaches hereto the Complainant's Letter, addressed to Chairmen Burr and Schiff, and the Classified Appendix. The ICIG has informed the Complainant that the transmittal of information by the Director of National Intelligence related to the Complainant's report to the congressional intelligence committees, as required by 50 U.S.C. § 3033(k)(5)(C), may not be limited to Chairmen Burr and Schiff.

(U) The Complainant's Letter and Classified Appendix delineate the Complainant's information pertaining to the urgent concern. According to the Complainant's Letter, "the actions described [in the Complainant's Letter and Classified Appendix] constitute 'a serious or flagrant problem, abuse, or violation of law or Executive Order,'" consistent with the definition of an "urgent concern" in 50 U.S.C. § 3033(k)(5)(G).

(U//FOUO) Upon receiving the information reported by the Complainant, the ICIG conducted a preliminary review to determine whether the report constituted "an urgent concern" under 50 U.S.C. § 3033(k)(5). As part of the preliminary review, the ICIG confirmed that the Complainant is "[a]n employee of an element of the intelligence community, an employee

---

[4] (U) *Id.* at § 3033(k)(5)(G)(i).

[5] (U) *Id.* at § 3033(g)(3)(A).

2

TOP SECRET/██████████████

assigned or detailed to an element of the intelligence community, or an employee of a contractor to the intelligence community."[6] The ICIG also confirmed that the Complainant intends to report to Congress the Complainant's information relating to the urgent concern.[7]

(TS/██████) As stated above, to constitute an "urgent concern" under 50 U.S.C. § 3033(k)(5)(G)(i), the information reported by the Complainant must constitute "[a] serious or flagrant problem, abuse, violation of law or Executive order, or deficiency relating to the funding, administration, or operation of an intelligence activity within the responsibility and authority of the Director of National Intelligence involving classified information."[8] Here, the Complainant's Letter alleged, among other things, that the President of the United States, in a telephone call with Ukrainian President Volodymyr Zelenskyy on July 25, 2019, "sought to pressure the Ukrainian leader to take actions to help the President's 2020 reelection bid." U.S. laws and regulations prohibit a foreign national, directly or indirectly, from making a contribution or donation of money or other thing of value, or to make an express or implied promise to make a contribution or donation, in connection with a Federal, State, or local election.[9] Similarly, U.S. laws and regulations prohibit a person from soliciting, accepting, or receiving such a contribution or donation from a foreign national, directly or indirectly, in connection with a Federal, State, or local election.[10] Further, in the ICIG's judgment, alleged conduct by a senior U.S. public official to seek foreign assistance to interfere in or influence a Federal election would constitute a "serious or flagrant problem [or] abuse" under 50 U.S.C. § 3033(k)(5)(G)(i), which would also potentially expose such a U.S. public official (or others acting in concert with the U.S. public official) to serious national security and counterintelligence risks with respect to foreign intelligence services aware of such alleged conduct.

(U) In addition, the Director of National Intelligence has responsibility and authority pursuant to federal law and Executive Orders to administer and operate programs and activities related to potential foreign interference in a United States election.[11] Among other

---

[6] (U) *Id.* at § 3033(k)(5)(A).

[7] (U) *Id.*

[8] (U) The Complainant's Classified Appendix appears to contain classified information involving an alleged "serious or flagrant problem, abuse, violation of law or Executive order, or deficiency relating to the funding, administration, or operation of an intelligence activity within the responsibility and authority of the Director of National Intelligence," as required by 50 U.S.C. § 3033(k)(5)(G)(i).

[9] (U) *See, e.g.,* 52 U.S.C. § 30121(a)(1)(A); 11 C.F.R. § 110.20(b).

[10] (U) *See, e.g.,* 52 U.S.C. § 30121(a)(2); 11 C.F.R. § 110.20(g).

[11] (U) *See, e.g.,* National Security Act of 1947, as amended; Exec. Order No. 12333, as amended, *United States Intelligence Activities;* Exec. Order No. 13848, *Imposing Certain Sanctions in the Event of Foreign Influence in a United States Election* (Sept. 12, 2018).

TOP SECRET/██████████████

3

responsibilities and authorities, subject to the authority, direction, and control of the President, the Director of National Intelligence "shall serve as the head of the Intelligence Community, act as the principal adviser to the President, to the [National Security Council], and to the Homeland Security Council for intelligence matters related to national security, and shall oversee and direct the implementation of the National Intelligence Program and execution of the National Intelligence Program budget."[12] Further, the United States Intelligence Community, "under the leadership of the Director [of National Intelligence]," shall "collect information concerning, and conduct activities to protect against, . . . intelligence activities directed against the United States."[13]

(U) More recently, in issuing Executive Order 13848, *Imposing Certain Sanctions in the Event of Foreign Influence in a United States Election* (Sept. 12, 2018), President Trump stated the following regarding foreign influence in United States elections:

> I, DONALD J. TRUMP, President of the United States of America, find that the ability of persons located, in whole or in part, outside the United States to interfere in or undermine public confidence in United States elections, including through the unauthorized accessing of election and campaign infrastructure or the covert distribution of propaganda and disinformation, constitutes an unusual and extraordinary threat to the national security and foreign policy of the United States.[14]

---

[12] (TS/███████) Exec. Order No. 12333 at § 1.3. In the Complainant's Classified Appendix, the Complainant reported that officials from the Office of Management and Budget, in the days before and on the day after the President's call on July 25, 2019, allegedly informed the "interagency" that the President had issued instructions to suspend all security assistance to Ukraine. The Complainant further alleges in the Classified Appendix that there might be a connection between the allegations concerning the substance of the President's telephone call with the Ukrainian President on July 25, 2019, and the alleged action to suspend (or continue the suspension of) all security assistance to Ukraine. If the allegedly improper motives were substantiated as part of a future investigation, the alleged suspension (or continued suspension) of all security assistance to Ukraine might implicate the Director of National Intelligence's responsibility and authority with regard to implementing the National Intelligence Program and/or executing the National Intelligence Program budget.

[13] (U) Exec. Order No. 12333 at § 1.4.

[14] (U) Among other directives, the Executive Order requires the Director of National Intelligence, in consultation with the heads of any other appropriate executive departments and agencies, not later than 45 days after the conclusion of a United States election, to "conduct an assessment of any information indicating that a foreign government, or any person acting as an agent of or on behalf of a foreign government, has acted with the intent or purpose of interfering in that election," and the "assessment shall identify, to the maximum extent ascertainable, the nature of any foreign interference and any methods employed to execute it, the persons involved, and the foreign government or governments that authorized, directed, sponsored, or supported it." Exec. Order No. 13848 at § 1.(a).

4

(U) Most recently, on July 19, 2019, as part of the Director of National Intelligence's responsibility and authority to administer and operate programs and activities related to potential foreign interference in a United States election, the Director of National Intelligence announced the establishment of the Intelligence Community Election Threats Executive. In the words of then-Director of National Intelligence Daniel R. Coats, who announced the establishment of the new position within the Office of the Director of National Intelligence (ODNI), "Election security is an enduring challenge and a top priority for the IC."[15] A few days later, in an internal announcement for the ODNI, then-Director Coats stated, "I can think of no higher priority mission than working to counter adversary efforts to undermine the very core of our democratic process."[16]

(U) As a result, I have determined that the Complainant's information would constitute an urgent concern, as defined in 50 U.S.C. § 3033(k)(5)(G)(i), provided that I also determine that the information "appears credible," as required by 50 U.S.C. § 3033(k)(5)(B).

(TS/██████) Based on the information reported by the Complainant to the ICIG and the ICIG's preliminary review, I have determined that there are reasonable grounds to believe that the complaint relating to the urgent concern "appears credible." The ICIG's preliminary review indicated that the Complainant has official and authorized access to the information and sources referenced in the Complainant's Letter and Classified Appendix, and that the Complainant has subject matter expertise related to much of the material information provided in the Complainant's Letter and Classified Appendix. The Complainant's Letter acknowledges that the Complainant was not a direct witness to the President's telephone call with the Ukrainian President on July 25, 2019. Other information obtained during the ICIG's preliminary review, however, supports the Complainant's allegation that, among other things, during the call the President "sought to pressure the Ukrainian leader to take actions to help the President's 2020 reelection bid." Further, although the ICIG's preliminary review identified some indicia of an arguable political bias on the part of the Complainant in favor of a rival political candidate, such evidence did not change my determination that the complaint relating to the urgent concern "appears credible," particularly given the other information the ICIG obtained during its preliminary review.

(TS/██████) As part of its preliminary review, the ICIG did not request access to records of the President's July 25, 2019, call with the Ukrainian President. Based on the sensitivity of the alleged urgent concern, I directed ICIG personnel to conduct a preliminary review of the Complainant's information. Based on the information obtained from the ICIG's preliminary review, I decided that access to records of the telephone call was not necessary to make my

---

[15] (U) ODNI News Release, *Director of National Intelligence Daniel R. Coats Establishes Intelligence Community Election Threats Executive* (July 19, 2019).

[16] (U) Memorandum from Daniel R. Coats, Director of National Intelligence, entitled, *Designation of Intelligence Community Election Threats Executive and Assistant Deputy Director for Mission Integration* (July 23, 2019).

determination that the complaint relating to the urgent concern "appears credible." In addition, given the time consumed by the preliminary review, together with lengthy negotiations that I anticipated over access to and use of records of the telephone call, particularly for purposes of communicating a disclosure to the congressional intelligence committees, I concluded that it would be highly unlikely for the ICIG to obtain those records within the limited remaining time allowed by the statute. I also understood from the ICIG's preliminary review that the National Security Council had already implemented special handling procedures to preserve all records of the telephone call.

(~~TS~~/██████) Nevertheless, the ICIG understands that the records of the call will be relevant to any further investigation of this matter. For your information, the ICIG has sent concurrently with this transmittal a notice of a document access request and a document hold notice to the White House Counsel to request access to and the preservation of any and all records related to the President's telephone call with the Ukrainian President on July 25, 2019, and alleged related efforts to solicit, obtain, or receive assistance from foreign nationals in Ukraine, directly or indirectly, in connection with a Federal election. The document access request and document hold notice were issued pursuant to the ICIG's authority to conduct independent investigations and reviews on programs and activities within the responsibility and authority of the Director of National Intelligence, which includes the authority for the ICIG to have "direct access to all records, reports, audits, reviews, documents, papers, recommendations, or other materials that relate to the programs and activities with respect to which the Inspector General has responsibilities under this section."[17]

(U) Having determined that the complaint relating to the urgent concern appears credible, I am transmitting to you this notice of my determination, along with the Complainant's Letter and Classified Appendix. Upon receipt of this transmittal, the Director of National Intelligence "shall, within 7 calendar days of such receipt, forward such transmittal to the congressional intelligence committees, together with any comments the Director considers appropriate."[18]

---

[17] (U) 50 U.S.C. § 3033(g)(2)(C). The ICIG's statutory right of access to those records is consistent with the statutory right of access to such records provided to the Director of National Intelligence. *See* 50 U.S.C. § 3024(b) ("Unless otherwise directed by the President, the Director of National Intelligence shall have access to all national intelligence and intelligence related to the national security which is collected by any Federal department, agency, or other entity, except as otherwise provided by law or, as appropriate, under guidelines agreed upon by the Attorney General and the Director of National Intelligence.").

[18] (U) *See* 50 U.S.C. § 3033(k)(5)(C). The ICIG notes that if the ICIG had determined the complaint was not an "urgent concern" or did not "appear[] credible," the statute would require the Director of National Intelligence to transmit the same information to the same congressional intelligence committees in the same time period, and provides the Complainant with the right "to submit the complaint or information to Congress by contacting either or both of the congressional intelligence committees directly," *id.* at § 3033(k)(5)(D)(i), subject to direction from the Director of National Intelligence, through the ICIG, "on how to contact the congressional intelligence committees in accordance with appropriate security practices," *id.* at § 3033(k)(5)(D)(ii).

6

Because the ICIG has the statutory responsibility to "notify an employee who reports a complaint or information" to the ICIG concerning an urgent concern "of each action taken" with respect to the complaint or information "not later than 3 days after any such action is taken,"[19] I respectfully request that you provide the ICIG with notice of your transmittal to the congressional intelligence committees not later than 3 days after the transmittal is made to them. In addition, as required by the statute, the ICIG is required to notify the Complainant not later than 3 days after today's date of my determination that the complaint relating to the urgent concern appears credible and that the ICIG transmitted on today's date notice of that determination to the Director of National Intelligence, along with the Complainant's Letter and Classified Appendix.

(U) If you have any questions or require additional information concerning this matter, please do not hesitate to contact me.

Sincerely yours,

Michael K. Atkinson
Inspector General
of the Intelligence Community

(U) Enclosures (Complainant's Letter and Classified Appendix) (Documents are ~~TS~~/██████████)

This Letter is ~~TOP SECRET~~/███████████████ when detached from the Enclosures

---

[19] (U) 50 U.S.C. § 3033(k)(5)(E).

7

3. The text of the phone conversation between President Trump and President Zelensky of Ukraine

UNCLASSIFIED

[PkgNumberShort]

Declassified by order of the President
September 24, 2019

MEMORANDUM OF TELEPHONE CONVERSATION

SUBJECT: ~~(C)~~ Telephone Conversation with President
                Zelenskyy of Ukraine

PARTICIPANTS: President Zelenskyy of Ukraine

                Notetakers: The White House Situation Room

DATE, TIME   July 25, 2019, 9:03 - 9:33 a.m. EDT
AND PLACE: Residence

~~(S/NF)~~ The President: Congratulations on a great victory. We all
watched from the United States and you did a terrific job. The
way you came from behind, somebody who wasn't given much of a
chance, and you ended up winning easily. It's a fantastic
achievement. Congratulations.

~~(S/NF)~~ President Zelenskyy: You are absolutely right Mr.
President. We did win big and we worked hard for this. We worked
a lot but I would like to confess to you that I had an
opportunity to learn from you. We used quite a few of your
skills and knowledge and were able to use it as an example for
our elections and yes it is true that these were unique
elections. We were in a unique situation that we were able to

CAUTION: A Memorandum of a Telephone Conversation (TELCON) is not a verbatim transcript of a
discussion. The text in this document records the notes and recollections of Situation Room Duty
Officers and NSC policy staff assigned to listen and memorialize the conversation in written form
as the conversation takes place. A number of factors can affect the accuracy of the record,
including poor telecommunications connections and variations in accent and/or interpretation.
The word "inaudible" is used to indicate portions of a conversation that the notetaker was unable
to hear.

Classified By: 2354726
Derived From: NSC SCG
Declassify On: 20441231

UNCLASSIFIED

2 **UNCLASSIFIED**

achieve a unique success. I'm able to tell you the following; the first time, you called me to congratulate me when I won my presidential election, and the second time you are now calling me when my party won the parliamentary election. I think I should run more often so you can call me more often and we can talk over the phone more often.

(S/NF) The President: [laughter] That's a very good idea. I think your country is very happy about that.

(S/NF) President Zelenskyy: Well yes, to tell you the truth, we are trying to work hard because we wanted to drain the swamp here in our country. We brought in many many new people. Not the old politicians, not the typical politicians, because we want to have a new format and a new type of government. You are a great teacher for us and in that.

(S/NF) The President: Well it's very nice of you to say that. I will say that we do a lot for Ukraine. We spend a lot of effort and a lot of time. Much more than the European countries are doing and they should be helping you more than they are. Germany does almost nothing for you. All they do is talk and I think it's something that you should really ask them about. When I was speaking to Angela Merkel she talks Ukraine, but she doesn't do anything. A lot of the European countries are the same way so I think it's something you want to look at but the United States has been very very good to Ukraine. I wouldn't say that it's reciprocal necessarily because things are happening that are not good but the United States has been very very good to Ukraine.

(S/NF) President Zelenskyy: Yes you are absolutely right. Not only 100%, but actually 1000% and I can tell you the following; I did talk to Angela Merkel and I did meet with her. I also met and talked with Macron and I told them that they are not doing quite as much as they need to be doing on the issues with the sanctions. They are not enforcing the sanctions. They are not working as much as they should work for Ukraine. It turns out that even though logically, the European Union should be our biggest partner but technically the United States is a much bigger partner than the European Union and I'm very grateful to you for that because the United States is doing quite a lot for Ukraine. Much more than the European Union especially when we are talking about sanctions against the Russian Federation. I would also like to thank you for your great support in the area of defense. We are ready to continue to cooperate for the next steps specifically we are almost ready to buy more Javelins from the United States for defense purposes.

UNCLASSIFIED

3

(S/NF) The President: I would like you to do us a favor though because our country has been through a lot and Ukraine knows a lot about it. I would like you to find out what happened with this whole situation with Ukraine, they say Crowdstrike... I guess you have one of your wealthy people... The server, they say Ukraine has it. There are a lot of things that went on, the whole situation. I think you're surrounding yourself with some of the same people. I would like to have the Attorney General call you or your people and I would like you to get to the bottom of it. As you saw yesterday, that whole nonsense ended with a very poor performance by a man named Robert Mueller, an incompetent performance, but they say a lot of it started with Ukraine. Whatever you can do, it's very important that you do it if that's possible.

(S/NF) President Zelenskyy: Yes it is very important for me and everything that you just mentioned earlier. For me as a President, it is very important and we are open for any future cooperation. We are ready to open a new page on cooperation in relations between the United States and Ukraine. For that purpose, I just recalled our ambassador from United States and he will be replaced by a very competent and very experienced ambassador who will work hard on making sure that our two nations are getting closer. I would also like and hope to see him having your trust and your confidence and have personal relations with you so we can cooperate even more so. I will personally tell you that one of my assistants spoke with Mr. Giuliani just recently and we are hoping very much that Mr. Giuliani will be able to travel to Ukraine and we will meet once he comes to Ukraine. I just wanted to assure you once again that you have nobody but friends around us. I will make sure that I surround myself with the best and most experienced people. I also wanted to tell you that we are friends. We are great friends and you Mr. President have friends in our country so we can continue our strategic partnership. I also plan to surround myself with great people and in addition to that investigation, I guarantee as the President of Ukraine that all the investigations will be done openly and candidly. That I can assure you.

(S/NF) The President: Good because I heard you had a prosecutor who was very good and he was shut down and that's really unfair. A lot of people are talking about that, the way they shut your very good prosecutor down and you had some very bad people involved. Mr. Giuliani is a highly respected man. He was the mayor of New York City, a great mayor, and I would like him to

4   UNCLASSIFIED

call you. I will ask him to call you along with the Attorney
General. Rudy very much knows what's happening and he is a very
capable guy. If you could speak to him that would be great. The
former ambassador from the United States, the woman, was bad
news and the people she was dealing with in the Ukraine were bad
news so I just want to let you know that. The other thing,
There's a lot of talk about Biden's son, that Biden stopped the
prosecution and a lot of people want to find out about that so
whatever you can do with the Attorney General would be great.
Biden went around bragging that he stopped the prosecution so if
you can look into it... It sounds horrible to me.

~~(S/NF)~~ President Zelenskyy: I wanted to tell you about the
prosecutor. First of all I understand and I'm knowledgeable
about the situation. Since we have won the absolute majority in
our Parliament, the next prosecutor general will be 100% my
person, my candidate, who will be approved by the parliament and
will start as a new prosecutor in September. He or she will look
into the situation, specifically to the company that you
mentioned in this issue. The issue of the investigation of the
case is actually the issue of making sure to restore the honesty
so we will take care of that and will work on the investigation
of the case. On top of that, I would kindly ask you if you have
any additional information that you can provide to us, it would
be very helpful for the investigation to make sure that we
administer justice in our country with regard to the Ambassador
to the United States from Ukraine as far as I recall her name
was Ivanovich. It was great that you were the first one who told
me that she was a bad ambassador because I agree with you 100%.
Her attitude towards me was far from the best as she admired the
previous President and she was on his side. She would not accept
me as a new President well enough.

~~(S/NF)~~ The President: Well, she's going to go through some
things. I will have Mr. Giuliani give you a call and I am also
going to have Attorney General Barr call and we will get to the
bottom of it. I'm sure you will figure it out. I heard the
prosecutor was treated very badly and he was a very fair
prosecutor so good luck with everything. Your economy is going
to get better and better I predict. You have a lot of assets.
It's a great country. I have many Ukrainian friends, their
incredible people.

~~(S/NF)~~ President Zelenskyy: I would like to tell you that I also
have quite a few Ukrainian friends that live in the United
States. Actually last time I traveled to the United States, I
stayed in New York near Central Park and I stayed at the Trump

UNCLASSIFIED

5 **UNCLASSIFIED**

Tower. I will talk to them and I hope to see them again in the future. I also wanted to thank you for your invitation to visit the United States, specifically Washington DC. On the other hand, I also want to ensure you that we will be very serious about the case and will work on the investigation. As to the economy, there is much potential for our two countries and one of the issues that is very important for Ukraine is energy independence. I believe we can be very successful and cooperating on energy independence with United States. We are already working on cooperation. We are buying American oil but I am very hopeful for a future meeting. We will have more time and more opportunities to discuss these opportunities and get to know each other better. I would like to thank you very much for your support

~~(S/NF)~~ The President: Good. Well, thank you very much and I appreciate that. I will tell Rudy and Attorney General Barr to call. Thank you. Whenever you would like to come to the White House, feel free to call. Give us a date and we'll work that out. I look forward to seeing you.

~~(S/NF)~~ President Zelenskyy: Thank you very much. I would be very happy to come and would be happy to meet with you personally and get to know you better. I am looking forward to our meeting and I also would like to invite you to visit Ukraine and come to the city of Kyiv which is a beautiful city. We have a beautiful country which would welcome you. On the other hand, I believe that on September 1 we will be in Poland and we can meet in Poland hopefully. After that, it might be a very good idea for you to travel to Ukraine. We can either take my plane and go to Ukraine or we can take your plane, which is probably much better than mine.

~~(S/NF)~~ The President: Okay, we can work that out. I look forward to seeing you in Washington and maybe in Poland because I think we are going to be there at that time.

~~(S/NF)~~ President Zelenskyy: Thank you very much Mr. President.

~~(S/NF)~~ The President: Congratulations on a fantastic job you've done. The whole world was watching. I'm not sure it was so much of an upset but congratulations.

~~(S/NF)~~ President Zelenskyy: Thank you Mr. President bye-bye.

-- End of Conversation --

UNCLASSIFIED

4. All tweets by President Trump from September 21, 2019 (7:31 am) to September 26 (11:48 pm)

1. <u>Sep 26, 2019 11:48:21 AM</u>Adam Schiff has zero credibility. Another fantasy to hurt the Republican Party!

2. <u>Sep 26, 2019 11:43:07 AM</u>A whistleblower with second hand information? Another Fake News Story! See what was said on the very nice, no pressure, call. Another Witch Hunt!

3. <u>Sep 26, 2019 11:37:35 AM</u>That, and many other reasons, is why Republicans will win North Carolina! https://t.co/m4GNvbp7oK

4. <u>Sep 26, 2019 11:21:10 AM</u>"Is there a case for impeachment? Absolutely not! There is no high crime or misdemeanor, no crime, no extortion, no treason." Robert Ray @FoxNews

5. <u>Sep 26, 2019 08:19:35 AM</u>"Is their a case for impeachment? Absolutely not!" There is no high crimes or misdemeanors, no treason, no extortion, no treason." RD Robert Ray, respected

6. <u>Sep 26, 2019 07:41:20 AM</u>THE DEMOCRATS ARE TRYING TO DESTROY THE REPUBLICAN PARTY AND ALL THAT IT STANDS FOR. STICK TOGETHER, PLAY THEIR GAME, AND FIGHT HARD REPUBLICANS. OUR COUNTRY IS AT STAKE!

7. <u>Sep 26, 2019 07:35:13 AM</u>RT @DonaldJTrumpJr: For 2.5 years we were told there was collusion, then obstruction, then it was a cover-up... rinse and repeat. Seems t...

8. <u>Sep 26, 2019 07:34:35 AM</u>RT @GeraldoRivera: After 3 years of relentless pursuit of @realDonaldTrump-@RepAdamSchiff (not various Democratic candidates for @POTUS) wi...

9. <u>Sep 26, 2019 07:34:06 AM</u>RT @ericbolling: The downright "giddy" media hoping for @realDonaldTrump impeachment should take 3 minutes and watch this before they count...

10. <u>Sep 26, 2019 07:32:46 AM</u>RT @TeamTrump: VP @mike_pence: Democrats don't have an agenda, that's why they want to impeach @realDonaldTrump https://t.co/El9qOb6bkq

11. <u>Sep 26, 2019 07:32:16 AM</u>RT @TeamTrump: Stop what you're doing... WATCH us expose the #FakeNews Media LIES about @realDonaldTrump! They selectively deleted 500+ w...

12. <u>Sep 26, 2019 07:27:14 AM</u>RT @VP: Tune in tonight as I join @LouDobbs! https://t.co/JOKvCtY3bM

13. <u>Sep 26, 2019 07:26:27 AM</u>RT @realDonaldTrump: So bad for our Country! https://t.co/BzlCeKn8hY

14. <u>Sep 26, 2019 07:25:45 AM</u>RT @realDonaldTrump: So true, but it will never work! https://t.co/UEi4U4lpTs

15. <u>Sep 26, 2019 07:25:17 AM</u>RT @Scavino45: https://t.co/Jm5JdYcKml

16. <u>Sep 26, 2019 07:21:26 AM</u>RT @JesseBWatters: When @realDonaldTrump became president, his sons stopped doing international business deals; when Joe Biden became VP, h...

17. <u>Sep 26, 2019 07:20:37 AM</u>RT @DonaldJTrumpJr: Yikes! I guess the Dems no longer want to do anything about election interference. https://t.co/X52fMO3CRj

18. Sep 26, 2019 07:19:56 AMRT @DonaldJTrumpJr: Rand Paul on the Fake Witch Hunts: BAS-TA! https://t.co/WNEsrU5XUM

19. Sep 26, 2019 07:19:44 AMRT @KellyannePolls: "Pelosi's Bad Impeachment Call" by anti-Trumper in @NYT. "A Q-PAC poll found 57% of Americans oppose impeachment; 37%...

20. Sep 26, 2019 07:18:59 AMRT @JesseBWatters: President @realDonaldTrump has taken a sledgehammer to the ruiling class and the ruling class is fighting back hard and...

21. Sep 26, 2019 07:05:07 AMRT @VP: ...They can't run against this President's record...a record of accomplishment...so they decided to look for one more way to try to...

22. Sep 26, 2019 07:04:38 AMRT @realDonaldTrump: https://t.co/hkl6Su3hSR

23. Sep 26, 2019 07:03:50 AMRT @VP: ...and even though she knew the transcript was going to be released today, Speaker Nancy Pelosi initiates an impeachment inquiry into...

24. Sep 26, 2019 07:02:40 AMRT @VP: The ironic thing is that the only time it did happen that we know about is when former Vice President Joe Biden threatened over a b...

25. Sep 26, 2019 07:00:44 AMRT @Jim_Jordan: Dems are basing their impeachment dreams on a "whistleblower" who: -Did not have direct knowledge of the Ukraine call -Had...

26. Sep 26, 2019 07:00:24 AMRT @RepChuck: Speaker Pelosi: Focused on taking down @realDonaldTrump at any cost. @POTUS: Focused on securing better trade deals for hard...

27. Sep 26, 2019 06:59:58 AMRT @KellyannePolls: cc: Everybody not the Ukranian President who has been characterizing what happened in the call with the Ukrainian Presi...

28. Sep 26, 2019 06:59:31 AMRT @CBSNews: Ukrainian President Volodymyr Zelensky says he doesn't want to be involved in US elections and he didn't feel "pushed" during...

29. Sep 26, 2019 06:24:29 AMTHE GREATEST SCAM IN THE HISTORY OF AMERICAN POLITICS!

30. Sep 26, 2019 06:20:00 AMRT @realDonaldTrump: https://t.co/U4PIG5LPIX

31. Sep 26, 2019 06:19:31 AMRT @realDonaldTrump: https://t.co/VmHKZpuPs4

32. Sep 26, 2019 06:18:31 AMRT @DonaldJTrumpJr: 😂😂😂 We should impeach them all. That's how this works, right? Given their rules its a no brainer since there's an actua...

33. Sep 26, 2019 06:17:58 AMRT @DonaldJTrumpJr: KASSAM: Trump Transcript Shows Him Trying To Stop Corruption, Nothing Else https://t.co/nEgLq8pITV via @dailycaller

34. Sep 26, 2019 06:17:02 AMThank you Jim! https://t.co/9ldr6iSdpl

35. Sep 26, 2019 06:15:49 AMRT @realDonaldTrump: "Democrats wrote to the Ukrainian government in May 2018 urging it to continue investigations into President Donald Tr...

36. Sep 26, 2019 06:15:22 AMRT @DonaldJTrumpJr: Yikes!!! https://t.co/uxleBmTtRl

37. Sep 26, 2019 06:15:12 AMRT @DonaldJTrumpJr: Are you saying the Democrats started an all out move towards impeachment without even seeing the transcript? https://t....

38. Sep 26, 2019 06:14:41 AMIf they actually did this the markets would crash. Do you think it

was luck that got us to the best Stock Market and Economy in our history. It wasn't! https://t.co/V0WGVWEWTN

39. Sep 26, 2019 06:09:42 AMRT @DonaldJTrumpJr: Watching the media circle the wagons and desperately try to defend the Biden family for things they try to kill my fami...

40. Sep 26, 2019 06:09:26 AMRT @realDonaldTrump: "The Democrats have been talking about Impeaching Donald Trump since before he was inaugurated." @SteveDoocy @foxandf...

41. Sep 26, 2019 06:08:44 AMSo bad for our Country! https://t.co/BzICeKn8hY

42. Sep 26, 2019 06:06:50 AMSo cute! Her father is under siege, for no reason, since his first day in office! https://t.co/8wtB3H4fth

43. Sep 26, 2019 06:03:30 AMRT @RealSaavedra: NEW: Democrat Senators reached out to Ukraine in May 2018 and asked for their assistance in investigating Trump "In the...

44. Sep 26, 2019 06:03:12 AMRT @AriFleischer: "Hunter took the position with a Ukrainian natural gas company just a few weeks after his father visited Ukraine in 2014...

45. Sep 26, 2019 06:01:39 AMRT @realDonaldTrump: There has been no President in the history of our Country who has been treated so badly as I have. The Democrats are f...

46. Sep 26, 2019 06:00:45 AMRT @realDonaldTrump: Thank you @kevinomccarthy! https://t.co/DhcGpWEOME

47. Sep 26, 2019 06:00:36 AMRT @realDonaldTrump: Sooooo true @LindseyGrahamSC! https://t.co/ZzFwXHV5ua

48. Sep 25, 2019 09:46:57 PMOne of our best fundraising days EVER! https://t.co/zohH8Xm5ak

49. Sep 25, 2019 09:45:46 PMSo true, but it will never work! https://t.co/UEi4U4lpTs

50. Sep 25, 2019 08:46:57 PMhttps://t.co/o88dILO9oU

51. Sep 25, 2019 04:34:00 PMhttps://t.co/hkl6Su3hSR

52. Sep 25, 2019 03:17:32 PMI have informed @GOPLeader Kevin McCarthy and all Republicans in the House that I fully support transparency on so-called whistleblower information but also insist on transparency from Joe Biden and his son Hunter, on the millions of dollars that have been quickly and easily....

53. Sep 25, 2019 03:17:32 PM....taken out of Ukraine and China. Additionally, I demand transparency from Democrats that went to Ukraine and attempted to force the new President to do things that they wanted under the form of political threat.

54. Sep 25, 2019 01:13:43 PMWow! "Ukraine Whistleblower's lead attorney donated to Biden." @FreeBeacon

55. Sep 25, 2019 12:54:43 PMRT @SenThomTillis: Nancy Pelosi should be embarrassed. The transcript debunks the Democrats' false claims against President @realDonaldTrum...

56. Sep 25, 2019 12:53:45 PMRT @jmclghln: 66-29 huge majority believes the Democrats should work w/ [LRI]@realDonaldTrump[PDI] to solve the nations problems rather than imp...

57. Sep 25, 2019 12:46:30 PMRT @RepRickAllen: Since the day President Trump was elected

to office, Democrats have tried to find any opportunity to undermine his presid...

58. Sep 25, 2019 12:46:13 PMRT @KimStrassel: 1) Having read DOJ's Trump-Ukraine release, here's the real story: This is another internal attempt to take out a presiden...

59. Sep 25, 2019 12:45:54 PMRT @SteveScalise: Dems launched an impeachment inquiry based on a rumor instead of waiting for the facts. It's now clear: there was no qui...

60. Sep 25, 2019 12:45:48 PMRT @EricTrump: "...involving an industry and business he knew nothing about." It is an absolute joke. The only corruption worse than Biden'...

61. Sep 25, 2019 12:45:36 PMRT @RepJeffDuncan: None of what Democrats said happened on the call between @realDonaldTrump & Ukrainian President Zelensky was true. No qu...

62. Sep 25, 2019 12:44:59 PMRT @RepMarkGreen: Once again, Democrats reveal that impeachment is not really about our country, but about their own imperative to maintain...

63. Sep 25, 2019 12:44:01 PMRT @RepPeteKing: Nothing remotely impeachable in transcript. Ukrainian President brought up Giuliani before @POTUS Trump mentioned Biden. N...

64. Sep 25, 2019 12:43:27 PMRT @RepMarkMeadows: As the left now tries to move the goalposts, remember that for days, all we heard was that @realDonaldTrump offered qui...

65. Sep 25, 2019 12:43:13 PMRT @RepMattGaetz: Unprecedented and unpatriotic. Nancy Pelosi undermined the solemn duty of impeachment that a future House may have to un...

66. Sep 25, 2019 11:33:29 AMhttps://t.co/U4PIG5LPIX

67. Sep 25, 2019 11:06:15 AMhttps://t.co/VmHKZpuPs4

68. Sep 25, 2019 10:56:50 AM"He (President Trump) didn't specifically mention the explicit quid pro quo of...unless you investigate this...we're going to withhold military aid to you." Pamela Brown

69. Sep 25, 2019 10:32:16 AMhttps://t.co/enifgzhUdC

70. Sep 25, 2019 10:25:13 AM"You don't see a direct quid pro quo in this." @BretBaier

71. Sep 25, 2019 09:58:08 AM"Democrats wrote to the Ukrainian government in May 2018 urging it to continue investigations into President Donald Trump's alleged collusion with Russia in the 2016 presidential campaign — collusion later found NOT TO EXIST." https://t.co/wY-dRmpfddk

72. Sep 25, 2019 08:59:22 AMhttps://t.co/coIrRDN33G

73. Sep 25, 2019 08:17:46 AMWill the Democrats apologize after seeing what was said on the call with the Ukrainian President? They should, a perfect call - got them by surprise!

74. Sep 25, 2019 08:11:57 AM"The Democrats have been talking about Impeaching Donald Trump since before he was inaugurated." @SteveDoocy @foxandfriends And for no reason other than the great success we are having with the Economy, the Military, Vets, Tax and Regulation Cuts, HealthCare, and so much more!

75. Sep 25, 2019 07:48:02 AMRT @RepDougCollins: Speaker Pelosi's decree changes absolutely nothing. As I have been telling Chairman Nadler for weeks, merely claiming t...

76. Sep 25, 2019 07:47:42 AMRT @RepMarkMeadows: POTUS says he's releasing the full transcript of the Ukraine call, and amazingly Democrats now say the whistleblower co...

77. Sep 25, 2019 07:46:58 AMRT @joegooding: This "whistleblower" was found by the Intelligence Community IG to have a political bias against @POTUS @realDonaldTrump an...

78. Sep 25, 2019 06:24:02 AMThere has been no President in the history of our Country who has been treated so badly as I have. The Democrats are frozen with hatred and fear. They get nothing done. This should never be allowed to happen to another President. Witch Hunt!

79. Sep 25, 2019 06:14:03 AMGreat new book by the brilliant Andrew McCarthy, BALL OF COLLUSION, THE PLOT TO RIG AN ELECTION AND DESTROY A PRESIDENCY. Get it, and some other great new books which I will soon be recommending. They tell you about the Crooked Pols and the Witch Hunt that has now been exposed!

80. Sep 24, 2019 10:41:45 PMThank you @LouDobbs and @JudgeJeanine! https://t.co/LdfGF-vAJNF

81. Sep 24, 2019 10:37:24 PMThank you @kevinomccarthy! https://t.co/DhcGpWEOME

82. Sep 24, 2019 10:34:49 PM"He (Trump) has already been suffering from this type of a Witch Hunt since before his Inauguration. If it's not one thing, it's another. It's a DISGRACE!" @pnjaban @LouDobbs https://t.co/9I9kXo2B8V

83. Sep 24, 2019 10:17:40 PMSooooo true @LindseyGrahamSC! https://t.co/ZzFwXHV5ua

84. Sep 24, 2019 10:04:28 PMThank you @JennaEllisRives -- totally agree! https://t.co/n3GD-dAHLWh

85. Sep 24, 2019 09:55:52 PM"They (Dems) are scrambling for a theme and narrative. They've gone everywhere from Russian Hoax to Russian Collusion...and now they've come to this... they think they should have won the 2016 election, they think in their bizarre brains that they did..." https://t.co/xqYFEAzT8D

86. Sep 24, 2019 09:35:04 PM"Mark Levin: Media trying to protect Biden, ignoring MASSIVE DEMOCRAT SCANDAL" https://t.co/9lI7wHwQ7J

87. Sep 24, 2019 09:26:39 PM"Attorney For Anti-Trump 'Whistleblower' Worked For Hillary Clinton, Chuck Schumer" https://t.co/yxQ5obwB6K

88. Sep 24, 2019 06:17:48 PMhttps://t.co/OFMzlMWpv1

89. Sep 24, 2019 05:22:40 PMSecretary of State Pompeo recieved permission from Ukraine Government to release the transcript of the telephone call I had with their President. They don't know either what the big deal is. A total Witch Hunt Scam by the Democrats!

90. Sep 24, 2019 04:32:32 PMhttps://t.co/1KOSnHguW2

91. Sep 24, 2019 04:17:42 PMPRESIDENTIAL HARASSMENT!

92. Sep 24, 2019 04:14:05 PMThey never even saw the transcript of the call. A total Witch Hunt!

93. Sep 24, 2019 04:11:15 PMPelosi, Nadler, Schiff and, of course, Maxine Waters! Can you believe this?

94. Sep 24, 2019 04:08:01 PMSuch an important day at the United Nations, so much work and

so much success, and the Democrats purposely had to ruin and demean it with more break-ing news Witch Hunt garbage. So bad for our Country!

95. Sep 24, 2019 02:13:13 PMRT @GOP: 🔔Are YOU registered to vote?🔔 Today is #National-VoterRegistrationDay, make sure you are registered to vote! Let's KEEP AMERICA...

96. Sep 24, 2019 01:52:31 PMThe Democrats are so focused on hurting the Republican Party and the President that they are unable to get anything done because of it, including legis-lation on gun safety, lowering of prescription drug prices, infrastructure, etc. So bad for our Country!

97. Sep 24, 2019 01:51:25 PMTHANK YOU! https://t.co/Ne2LOSAWpX

98. Sep 24, 2019 01:12:11 PM....You will see it was a very friendly and totally appropriate call. No pressure and, unlike Joe Biden and his son, NO quid pro quo! This is nothing more than a continuation of the Greatest and most Destructive Witch Hunt of all time!

99. Sep 24, 2019 01:12:09 PMI am currently at the United Nations representing our Country, but have authorized the release tomorrow of the complete, fully declassified and unredacted transcript of my phone conversation with President Zelensky of Ukraine....

100. Sep 23, 2019 11:20:41 PMRT @RandPaul: .@realDonaldTrump is showing that real strength and statesmanship can coexist with restraint. America is unquestionably the m...

101. Sep 23, 2019 11:18:12 PMRT @cspan: Q: "You can authorize to release the tran-script. Will you do that?" President Trump: "I can do it very easily, but I'd rather n...

102. Sep 23, 2019 11:09:27 PMHopefully they will work it out, and quickly! https://t.co/J2JGz6mfCW

103. Sep 23, 2019 11:04:32 PMRT @cspan: President Trump: "I think I'll get a Nobel prize for a lot of things," https://t.co/XPRfWZyYc6

104. Sep 23, 2019 11:02:04 PMTrue. A wonderful meeting! https://t.co/W9ByXaS8Qf

105. Sep 23, 2019 10:55:29 PMRT @hogangidley45: "Today, it is my true honor to be the first President of the United States to host a meeting at the United Nations on re...

106. Sep 23, 2019 10:36:12 PMShe seems like a very happy young girl looking forward to a bright and wonderful future. So nice to see! https://t.co/1tQG6QcVKO

107. Sep 23, 2019 07:37:02 PMhttps://t.co/p5imhMJqS1

108. Sep 23, 2019 06:24:31 PM"@FoxNews bombshell information reports that the so-called Whistleblower did not have firsthand knowledge of that phone conversation with Ukraine's President." Wow! @HARRISFAULKNER It is all a Democrat/Adam Schiff Scam! Doing this for 3 years now, and found NOTHING!

109. Sep 23, 2019 06:15:15 PM#UNGA https://t.co/ilZugqjEhP

110. Sep 23, 2019 05:44:25 PM94% approval rating in the Republican Party. Thank you!

111. Sep 23, 2019 03:21:42 PMThank you, working hard! https://t.co/1CpxcJOtha

112. Sep 23, 2019 02:37:27 PMThis is the real corruption that the Fake News Media refuses to even acknowledge! https://t.co/FCvUtWA33j

113. Sep 23, 2019 01:57:35 PMRT @WhiteHouse: "With one clear voice, the United States of America calls on the nations of the world to end religious persecution." #UNGA...

114. Sep 23, 2019 01:57:29 PMRT @WhiteHouse: President @realDonaldTrump just delivered a critical message on religious freedom and global persecution. "Our founders un...

115. Sep 23, 2019 10:29:11 AM....know the correct facts. Is he on our Country's side. Where does he come from. Is this all about Schiff & the Democrats again after years of being wrong?

116. Sep 23, 2019 10:29:08 AM"The very thing that they are accusing President Trump of doing (which I didn't do), was actually done by Joe Biden. Continues to be a double standard." @RepDevinNunes @foxandfriends These people are stone cold Crooked. Also, who is this so-called "whistleblower" who doesn't...

117. Sep 22, 2019 10:03:47 PMhttps://t.co/lYQkgU9G04

118. Sep 22, 2019 07:06:54 PMJust leaving the Great State of Ohio for New York and a few big days at the United Nations. Your Country will be well represented!

119. Sep 22, 2019 07:03:56 PM..Breaking News: The Ukrainian Government just said they weren't pressured at all during the "nice" call. Sleepy Joe Biden, on the other hand, forced a tough prosecutor out from investigating his son's company by threat of not giving big dollars to Ukraine. That's the real story!

120. Sep 22, 2019 07:03:55 PMNow the Fake News Media says I "pressured the Ukrainian President at least 8 times during my telephone call with him." This supposedly comes from a so-called "whistleblower" who they say doesn't even have a first hand account of what was said. More Democrat/Crooked Media con.....

121. Sep 22, 2019 06:42:10 PMhttps://t.co/J7g5L8LzrV

122. Sep 22, 2019 04:27:46 PMRT @sanghaviharsh: He has already made the American economy strong again. He has achieved much for the US and for the world. We, in India...

123. Sep 22, 2019 02:05:45 PMIncredible! https://t.co/SHs0RkxjzF

124. Sep 22, 2019 02:03:37 PMThe USA Loves India! https://t.co/xIfnWafxpg

125. Sep 22, 2019 01:11:17 PMhttps://t.co/heZ2mNSBUw

126. Sep 22, 2019 10:34:01 AMJustice Kavanaugh should sue The Failing New York Times for all they are worth!

127. Sep 22, 2019 10:28:48 AMLook forward to being with our great India loving community! https://t.co/RIdaoFw0Uc

128. Sep 22, 2019 10:22:23 AM"The @nytimes is trying to make someone (Justice Kavanaugh) into an evil person when they don't have the information to back it up. It is a false hoax." @MZHemingway @MediaBuzzFNC Zero people were fired at the Times. Why?

129. Sep 22, 2019 09:39:53 AMWill be in Houston to be with my friend. Will be a great day in Texas! https://t.co/SqdOZfqd2b

130. Sep 22, 2019 09:29:04 AM"They are trying to destroy and influence Justice Kavanaugh, a very good man." @LindseyGrahamSC 100% correct, and they should be fully exposed for what they are!

131. Sep 22, 2019 08:39:34 AMRT @SteveScalise: Dems say they will impeach @realDonaldTrump, but have no reason. Dems say they won't ban guns, but their bills do just t...

132. Sep 22, 2019 08:39:21 AMI go along with Joe! https://t.co/zVxBruUYF8

133. Sep 22, 2019 08:39:20 AM"Go across the world and you'll see either very low interest rates, or negative rates. The President wants to be competitive with these other countries on this, but I don't think he'll fire Jay Powell (even if I should!)." We should always be paying less interest than others!

134. Sep 22, 2019 08:39:19 AM"The real story involves Hunter Biden going around the world and collecting large payments from foreign governments and foreign oligarchs." Peter Schweizer Laura Ingraham Hunter made a fortune in Ukraine and in China. He knew nothing about Energy, or anything else.

135. Sep 21, 2019 08:49:00 PMhttps://t.co/le48VOltE0

136. Sep 21, 2019 07:18:11 PMRT @WhiteHouse: President @realDonaldTrump took a firsthand look at border wall construction and received a progress update from Border Pat...

137. Sep 21, 2019 07:15:59 PM"When someone gets nominated overwhelmingly, and then wins the Election, as he did, then he gets to set the National Agenda. The press is just outrages. This @nytimes story is the most irresponsible thing I've ever seen." @EdRollins @LouDobbs I agree. They also lose too much!

138. Sep 21, 2019 07:04:46 PM...The Fake News Media nowadays not only doesn't check for the accuracy of the facts, they knowingly make up the facts. They even make up sources in order to protect their partners, the Democrats. It is so wrong, but they don't even care anymore. They have gone totally CRAZY!!!!

139. Sep 21, 2019 07:04:45 PMThe LameStream Media had a very bad week. They pushed numerous phony stories and got caught, especially The Failing New York Times, which has lost more money over the last 10 years than any paper in history, and The Amazon Washington Post. They are The Enemy of the People!

140. Sep 21, 2019 05:47:22 PM"Ukraine Foreign Minister disputes reports of any pressure from Trump. This conversation was long, friendly, and it touched on many questions." @NBCNews Correct. If your looking for something done wrong, just look at the tape of Sleepy Joe. He is being protected by the Media!

141. Sep 21, 2019 04:50:08 PM"They're trying to turn what was a Biden scandal into a Trump scandal." @PeterSchweizer The problem is, "Trump" did nothing wrong!

142. Sep 21, 2019 04:47:50 PM"It appears that an American spy in one of our intelligence agencies may have been spying on our own president. The complaint suggests that this intel agent was listening in on Trump's conversation....

143. Sep 21, 2019 04:47:50 PM....with a foreign leader. Was this person officially asked to listen to the conversation or was he or she secretly listening in?" @GreggJarrett

144. Sep 21, 2019 04:43:07 PM"The pretend Ukraine scandal is an another malicious seditious effort to protect the Obama/Clinton gang. Criminal classified leaks and spying targeting Trump — again." @TomFitton

145. Sep 21, 2019 04:38:54 PM"They're trying to turn what was a Biden scandal into a Trump scandal." @PeterScheeizer The problem is, "Trump" did nothing wrong!

146.　　　Sep 21, 2019 04:11:33 PMhttps://t.co/LfXqfVEvx1

147.　　　Sep 21, 2019 04:10:48 PMhttps://t.co/ytF18g7mL2

148.　　　Sep 21, 2019 02:32:26 PMRT @RepDougCollins: Friday FOIA dump confirms coup planned to take down @RealDonaldTrump, and McCabe used the FBI to pursue the collusion n...

149.　　　Sep 21, 2019 02:30:04 PMhttps://t.co/cdvbUMJxb9

150.　　　Sep 21, 2019 02:28:32 PMSome of the best Economic Numbers our Country has ever experienced are happening right now. This is despite a Crooked and Demented Deep State, and a probably illegal Democrat/Fake News Media Partnership the likes of which the world has never seen. MAKE AMERICA GREAT AGAIN!

151.　　　Sep 21, 2019 01:04:19 PMhttps://t.co/elXWfWK7Kt

152.　　　Sep 21, 2019 11:57:31 AMhttps://t.co/t6O2yJITc0

153.　　　Sep 21, 2019 09:02:16 AMNow that the Democrats and the Fake News Media have gone "bust" on every other of their Witch Hunt schemes, they are trying to start one just as ridiculous as the others, call it the Ukraine Witch Hunt, while at the same time trying to protect Sleepy Joe Biden. Will fail again!

154.　　　Sep 21, 2019 07:53:55 AMThis is the real and only story! https://t.co/4z8eOcm6PA

155.　　　Sep 21, 2019 07:31:36 AM....story about me and a perfectly fine and routine conversation I had with the new President of the Ukraine. Nothing was said that was in any way wrong, but Biden's demand, on the other hand, was a complete and total disaster. The Fake News knows this but doesn't want to report!

156.　　　Sep 21, 2019 07:31:35 AMThe Fake News Media and their partner, the Democrat Party, want to stay as far away as possible from the Joe Biden demand that the Ukrainian Government fire a prosecutor who was investigating his son, or they won't get a very large amount of U.S. money, so they fabricate a.....

www.ingramcontent.com/pod-product-compliance
Lightning Source LLC
Chambersburg PA
CBHW081724290326
41933CB00053B/3313